Porto

Travel Guide

Quick Trips Series

Table of Contents

Porto

Porto was registered as a World Heritage Site by UNESCO in 1996 and designated as the European Capital of Culture in 2001. In Portugal there is a local saying that 'while Lisbon lazes, Porto labors,' and while always living in the shadow of the capital, Porto is one of the oldest cities in Europe.

PORTO TRAVEL GUIDE

When holidaying in Portugal many people head south to the sunshine of the Algarve or to Lisbon. However a new major tourist city is emerging on the world stage. Welcome to Portugal's "second-city" of Porto!

Porto is known worldwide for its wine, beautiful bridges and its eye-catching architecture, (a mixture of old and contemporaneous).

Several old parts and establishments of the city have been lovingly restored during the past decade. Care has been taken to preserve their heritage.

The time has come to visit the city of Porto, the traveler who does will experience a unique city, a pleasant climate and the world capital of Port Wine. Just like when you taste some of the famous Port Wines, you should experience Porto slowly to experience her delights.

🌍 Customs & Culture

Despite being the second largest city in Portugal, Porto stills receives less foreign visitors than the southern regions of the country (800,000 tourists per year compared to 7 million per year in the Algarve). And this reflects in the fact that it is common to find people in Porto who can't speak or understand English at all.

However, many travelers describe it rather as a positive factor. 'It feels like we are actually visiting a real city instead of a place which only exists to serve tourist customers,' they say.

They also affirm that, because of the occasional mixture of languages while attempting to communicate and the friendliness of the Portuguese people, it is possible to view the city in a more local perspective and to properly experience Portugal's great traditions and customs.

There are many festivities celebrated in the city through the year, but the most ancient and famous fun event of all is Saint John's Day, which occurs from the 23rd to the 24th of July, when thousands of people invade the streets and celebrate through the night. But the city of Porto is much more than old traditions and each year the city hosts over 10,000 events, from theatre plays to expositions and club parties with famous DJs.

PORTO TRAVEL GUIDE

Another element which differentiates Porto (and Portugal in general) from the rest of Europe, is the low price of high quality hostels (starting at 10€, per night for a dorm room) and of life in general. As an example, a coffee in this caffeine-addicted country can be bought for 0.60 cents in Porto.

🌍 Geography

Porto is located in the North of Portugal (in the northwest of the Iberian Peninsula) and is about 275km North of Lisbon. Most people used to reach Porto by bus or train from the capital, but due to the recent expansion of the Porto Airport (located 11km North from the city), travelers from many countries are now able to arrive by direct flights.

PORTO TRAVEL GUIDE

The metro is the easiest way to reach the center of the city, but if the visitor carries heavy luggage it might be better to take a taxi (the cost of the ride sits between €20-€30) or, even better, pre-book a private arrival transfer for €12.25.

Once in the center of the city, most of the main sights can be found within walking distance (although the city is rather hilly), but if transportation is needed, the most common means is the metro, which runs from 6AM to 1AM and uses a wavy blue 'M' as a station marker. There are also two short tram routes still operating; No.1 – a pleasant ride along the riverfront all the way to Foz do Douro - and No.18. The trip ticket costs €2.50 and the ticket for a trip plus a visit to the Tram Museum is €4. You can also buy the unlimited 24 hour trip plus Museum visit ticket for €8.

The bus (which runs from 6AM to 9PM) may be needed if the traveler wants to reach the Casa de Musica, the Serralves Museum or the Foz district. The tickets cost between €1.20 and €3.80, although if you're planning to stay for a while, you can purchase the unlimited Andante Tour 1 ticket for 24 hours – €7 - or the Andante Tour 3 for 72 hours – €15. However, to visit the restaurants and clubs away from the center of the city at night, the visitor must take an inexpensive taxi ride.

🌏 Weather & Best Time to Visit

While being naturally cooler than the southern regions of Portugal, the city of Porto is embraced by the most-often lovely Portuguese climate.

In the winter season the temperatures usually stay between 5 and 14 degrees Celsius, seldom dropping below zero.

In this season the weather switches between showery and cold but cloudless days, so bring your umbrella and scarf, hat and gloves if you are planning a stay in Porto for the winter or in the early spring.

In the summer, the thermometer flucuates between 15 and 25 degrees with July and August being the hottest months. Occasionally the weather gets unpleasant when

it reaches 35 degrees Celsius but this isn't common,

owing to the proximity of the city to the sea. This would be

a great time for a Douro Valley trip (one of the world's

oldest wine regions). Watch out for occasional cool or

rainy periods in the summertime as well.

Sights & Activities: What to See & Do

🌐 Taste Port Wine on the Riverside at Cais da Gaia

Gaia riverfront (left bank of the Douro river)

http://www.caisdegaia.com/

Located across the Douro River from Porto, Cais de Gaia

is one of the best places to see (and photograph) the beautiful World Heritage skyline of Porto and the lovely fishing boats, the famous double height Dom Luis I Bridge and the Douro river itself. Visit during the day and after nightfall to witness its varied beauty.

Cais de Gaia is the center of the port wine trade with many famous wine lodges along the riverfront. The whole area has been transformed into a place of leisure and entertainment with many typical restaurants where traditional Portuguese food is served, as well as many serving international cuisines, such as Italian, Japanese, Brazilian, Spanish and Indian food.

It's in Gaia (which is a separate city but only a very short walk across the bridge from Porto) that most of the famous Port wine lodges are found. Many of them are open to the public with several offering guided tours and port wine tastings, explaining the origins and characteristics of the wine, the storage process and winemaking. The Port wine lodges are one of best attractions to experience when visiting Porto, and Port is one the most famous dessert wines in the world. Taylor's, Graham, Sandeman and Cockburn will sound familiar to Europeans and they are all here. Sandeman is one of the most accessible wineries (it stands right on the riverfront), and you can also take an adventure uphill to enjoy the various types of Port in the different lodges.

Sandeman Port Lodge

Largo Miguel Bombarda 3

Vila Nova de Gaia, 4400-222

Tel: +351 223 740 533 / 34 / 35

http://www.sandeman.eu/

Cockburn's Port Lodge

Rua D. Leonor de Freitas

Vila Nova de Gaia, 4400-123

Tel: +351 223 776 484

http://www.cockburns.com/

W & J Graham's Port Lodge

Rua Rei Ramiro 514

Vila Nova de Gaia, 4400-281

Tel: +351 223 776 484 / 85

http://www.grahams-port.com/

http://www.grahamsportlodge.com/

Experience the beauty of Porto by sitting with a newspaper and a cup of coffee on the Gaia waterfront and savouring the views of the city of Porto from across the river. In Cais de Gaia you can also take a cruise trip on the Douro River to explore the wineries and green, hilly vistas of Northern Portugal. Along Gaia's waterfront there are several bars, clubs and an Irish pub where you can relax during the day as well as party through the night.

View The Douro River & Bridges from Porto's Cais da Ribeira

Porto's Riverside (central area)

UNESCO declared this area a World Heritage Site, and visitors to Cais da Ribeira will see the reasons why. It's one the most ancient squares of the city (mentioned in documents dating from the 14th century). Ribeira's narrow streets, colorful ancient houses and traditional boats floating along the quayside provide picturesque views. Ribeira is a lovely area to stroll and perhaps to dine at one of the quality restaurants in an evening. The area is also a great spot for a drink during the day and for celebrating at night.

It is here that the whole city comes to on festivities such as the Saint John's Day and New Year's Eve to see the major firework displays over the river. Ribeira has dozens of cafés, restaurants, bars and the never-absent port wine lodges, and it is one of the most popular districts of Porto in which to eat and drink. Ribeira is a romantic district, especially at night, so bring your better half!

🌐 Museum of Transport & Communications

Alfândega Building

Rua Nova da Alfândega

Porto, 4050-430

Tel: +351 223 403 000

http://www.amtc.pt/

Sitting on the west riverbank of Cais da Ribeira, Porto's neoclassical Customs House – or Alfândega – was built in 1860 and is now a dynamic cultural space, as well as the location of the Museum of Transport and Communications.

 This contemporary Museum offers a better insight into the importance of transportation with its permanent exhibition named "Cars through the Ages". One of the main highlights is the Panhard & Levassor, the first car to enter Portugal, brought from Paris in 1895.

The other permanent exhibitions at the Museum are named 'Communicate' and 'Metamorphosis of a Place: The Customs Museum', this last one being held in memory of the Customs House Building in Porto (Alfândega) and to Customs Houses in general.

🌍 Tram Museum

Alameda Basílio Teles 51

Porto, 4050-127

Tel: +351 226 158 185

http://museudocarroelectrico.pt/

The Tram Museum shows an interesting collection of

trams and other vehicles that used to circulate across the city, such as a horse-drawn American tram which was used for the first time in Porto in 1872.

Situated in Massarelos' former power station, the Museum includes a power processing plant from the early 1900's. The Tram Museum offers a variety of events and tram rental services, entertainment and educational services and a documentation center. The trip to the Museum can be taken by hopping on Tram No.1, which circulates around Cais da Ribeira. Buy a ticket that includes a visit to the Tram Museum for €4 (€2.50 for children 4-12 years old and 0-4 year olds travel for free).

🌑 Crystal Palace Gardens

Rua D. Manuel II

Porto, 4050-346

These romantic gardens were designed by the German landscaper Émile David in the former Crystal Palace, which was replaced by the Rosa Mota Pavilion in the 1950's. The area is currently used to host concerts and sports events.

The gardens cover 23.5 acres of land, consisting of many different gardens, such as the Émilio David Garden – containing beautiful fountains and allusive statues to the seasons of the year – as well as the theme gardens – the Herbs Garden, the Twinned Towns Garden and the Feelings Garden. Other gardens areas worth seeing are the Grove, the Indian-Chestnut-Tree Avenue and the Rose Garden, which shows aspects of the artistic heritage of the city. Nearby it is possible to see seven examples of Californian Palm Trees.

One of the most outstanding sights in the gardens is Linden Trees Avenue. This area is surrounded by the Almeida Garret Library, the Acoustic Shell Auditorium and the Charles Albert of Sardinia Chapel. A restaurant and an esplanade overlooking the pond can be found nearby, along with several viewpoints – also available all over the Gardens – which offers panoramic views of the Douro River and the city.

🌐 Romantic Museum

Rua Entre-Quintas 220

Porto, 4050-240

Tel: +351 226 057 000

The bucolic surroundings, including the garden, the grove

and the former farmer land, lend this Museum a romantic

environment. The goal of the Romantic Museum is to

recreate the household atmosphere of the 19th century

bourgeoisie living in Porto. Charles Albert, King of

Piedmont and Sardinia, stayed here in exile for his final

days until he died in 1849.

In honor of the King, some of the house's facilities such

as the Chapel, the bedroom and the living room were

rebuilt from watercolor paintings and lithographs from that

period. Also, one of the highlights of the Museum is the

Canvases Room, which gathers huge tempera-painted

canvases portraying episodes of typical Romantic ruins.

Bolhão Market

Rua Formosa

Porto, 4000-214

Tel: +315 223 326 024

Being the most famous and ancient market in the city,

dating back to 1850, the Bolhão Market is the place to buy

everything from fresh fruit to bread, flowers, vegetables,

meat, fish and even household goods.

Characterized by the monumentality of its neoclassical

architecture, the two-story building is divided into a great number of shops, facing the four surrounding streets –

Alexandre Braga (to the East), Formosa (to the South),

Sá da Bandeira (to the West) and Fernandes Tomás (to

the North).

Classified as a place of public interest, it is remarkable for

the noisy and exuberant atmosphere. One of the most

entertaining highlights in the market is hearing the

extravagant fishwives hawking the freshest catch in

authentic Porto style. Come here to experience

Portuguese traditions and to talk with the interesting

locals at work and to feel the embrace of Portuguese life.

🌐 Serralves Museum of Contemporary Art

Rua D. João Castro 210

Porto, 4150-417

Tel: +351 226 156 500

http://serralves.pt/

The striking minimalist building designed by the Pritzker Prize-winning architect Alvaro Siza Vieira is just the start of the adventure at this world-class museum. It is the first project of its kind in Portugal, with the mission of raising the public's awareness of the subject of contemporary art and the environment, and it is currently the most visited paid museum in the country.

The cutting-edge contemporary art at the Serralves museum is temporarily displayed rather than on permanent exhibition, but each collection takes up the entire space, along with that of the separate pink Art Deco construction – Casa de Serralves – located in the surrounding gardens (which are magnificent and also worthy of a visit themselves). Major displays in the past have included 'Paula Rego', 'Francis Bacon, Caged-Uncaged' and 'Andy Warhol: a Factory'.

If you are visiting Porto in late May or early June, make sure you visit the museum's annual festival 'Serralves em Festa', offering 40 hours of free contemporary art and culture allusive events. Also, don't forget to stop by the museum shop for the best in Portuguese design.

🌎 Casa da Musica

Avenida da Boavista 604

Porto, 4149-071

Tel: +351 220 120 220

http://www.casadamusica.com/

Inaugurated in 2005, this irregular-shaped twelve-story building was designed by the Dutch architect Rem Koolhaas exclusively for musical performances. Casa da Musica houses 1,300 in a perfectly acoustic auditorium and also offers a VIP room. It has become an example of contemporary architecture since, and many travel from all over the world to enjoy a guided tour at Casa da Musica or to attend the performances.

The dynamic and innovative programming ranges from urban trends to classical music, benefiting from the four different front groups: Choir, Symphony Orchestra, Remix Ensemble and Baroque Orchestra. Casa da Musica also promotes workshops, concerts and several other activities for children, families and schools.

In the recommended guided tour, visitors will be shown

the various components of the building and they can

interact with the equipment/instruments on display to the

public. You can also enjoy of several bars and a

restaurant located on the rooftop of the institution, which

provides a magnificent view overlooking the city.

🌐 São Francisco Church

Rua do Infante D. Henrique

Porto, 4050-297

Tel: +351 222 062 100

From the outside it might seem like an ordinary 14th

century Baroque and Gothic construction, but on the

inside it has one of the most fabulous and opulent church interiors in all of Europe. The gilt wood carvings, marble and pure gold decoration (the church contains 400kg of gold) date back to the 17th and 18th centuries and the church was classified as a National Monument in 1910.

The church no longer holds church services, but classical music concerts are often performed here. There is also a museum located in the catacombs below comprising artifacts from the former abbey. If you only have the time to visit one church in Porto, make it this one.

🌍 Carmo Church

Rua do Carmo

Porto, 4050-164

PORTO TRAVEL GUIDE

Tel: +351 222 078 400

What, at first sight, seems like one great church is actually two different churches, separated by what is one of the World's narrowest houses – only 1 meter wide! The house was built according to a law which stated that two churches could never share a wall, probably to ensure the chastity between the monks of Carmo Church and the nuns of Carmelita's. The narrow house was actually inhabited until roughly 20 years ago.

On the left side you can visit Carmelitas Church which is part of a 17th century former monastery with a bell tower, a richly gilded interior and a classical façade. It is on the right that tourists head more frequently, to Carmo Church.

Carmo Church is a late 18th century's construction, considered to be one of Porto rococo's most remarkable buildings. It is a great example of late baroque architecture and has a single nave by Francisco Pereira Campanhã with unique gilt carvings on seven altars.

On the outside of the Church you can see hand painted tiles on the lateral façade. In 1912 the tiles' paintings were designed by Silvester Silvestri and painted by Carlos Branco. On the tiles are represented episodes of the foundation of Mount Carmel and the Order of Carmelites.

🌐 Foz do Douro (Foz District)

Western Porto

One of the most sophisticated districts in Porto, Foz do

PORTO TRAVEL GUIDE

Douro is the perfect place to lounge by the seaside in its cafés, bars, restaurants and clubs overlooking the ocean. The area of Brazil Avenue, facing the sea, provides a resort-like atmosphere with wide-open spaces, beaches, esplanades and large attractive houses.

The waterfront cafés preserve their popularity even during the winter and this area is the venue where the locals come to skate, ride a bike, jog and socialize, Sunday mornings being their favorite time to do so.

Most of the beaches at Foz do Douro are not recommended for swimming, as the ocean has outcrops of rocks, but they are certainly a great escape from the city.

🌐 Passeio Alegre Garden

Rua do Passeio Alegre

Foz do Douro

Porto, 4150

A walk through the Passeio Alegre Gardens, which feature two obelisks from the 19th century, palm trees, sculptures, a bandstand where philharmonic concerts are performed during the summer, two mini-golf courses, a pond and a fountain. The construction of the Garden was by the same landscaper who designed the Crystal Palace Gardens, Émile David, in the late nineteenth century.

🌐 City Park

Avenida da Boavista

Porto

PORTO TRAVEL GUIDE

After walking a little over 2 miles along the beaches you will reach City Park. It is the largest urban park in Portugal, occupying about 200 acres and containing about 8.5km of paths. The park has aesthetic influences from several European gardens built since the seventeen hundreds.

It is filled with small groves, spacious lawns, ponds, animals, aquatic vegetation, benches and tables and it is common to find locals exercising as well as families and couples picnicking in the shady spots of the garden. It is, in fact, the perfect place to take a deep breath and get in contact with the natural world.

🌐 Lello Book Store

Rua das Carmelitas 144

Porto, 4050-161

Tel: +351 222 018 170

Lello Book Store was inaugurated in 1906 in a beautiful library and it still there today. The lovely Art Nouveau façade has neo-gothic details and the interior of the library is decorated in plaster that has been painted to imitate wood. The main highlight of the building is the magnificent staircase leading to the upper floor and the huge stained-glass skylight, displaying the store's monogram and its motto 'Decus in Labore', meaning 'Pride in Labor'. The Guardian and Lonely Planet considered Lello Library the third most beautiful in the world and described it as an 'Art Nouveau gem'.

Most of the books in the library are in Portuguese, but there are sections of publications written in English and several other languages, and the owners of the store claim that at least 80% of the people who enter the shop buy a book as a souvenir. The library is closed on Sunday so make sure to include it in your weekday plans, or, if you're in Porto only for the weekend, stop by on a Saturday before 7pm. Free entry.

● Majestic Café

Rua Santa Catarina 112

Porto, 4000-442

Tel: +351 222 003 887

http://cafemajestic.com/

An original building from 1921, with its original name 'Elite' soon changed to the current name, Majestic, is a World Heritage Site. It has been named on the Top 10 Most Beautiful Cafés in the World list by ucityguides.

The café was restored and it was reopened in 1994. The Majestic's architecture is from Belle Époque times and is luxurious and filled with chandeliers and with mirrors decorated with cherubs, wood and marble.

The café hosts many famous figures, both Portuguese and international. In J. K. Rowling's biography written by Sean Smith, it describes how, when the British writer lived in Porto, she would visit the café while working on her first Harry Potter book.

Also a gourmet restaurant, the Majestic's menus are mouth-watering. Customers can start the day with a premium breakfast menu and between 3 and 7pm they can enjoy the Majestic Tea, which is their version of a British high tea, with sandwiches and pastries. The meal courses are a variety of traditional, original and foreign dishes, all of them with a gourmet touch at this glamorous restaurant. There are also special menus for Valentine's Day and Carnival.

If you are planning on dining at the Majestic during your trip to Porto reserve a table in advance. You can do that through their website or by phone.

☺ Avenida dos Aliados

City center

The heart of the city was renovated in 2006 by the same architect who designed the Serralves Museum. The avenue consists of grand buildings with interesting architecture including details such as skyline crowns, pinnacles and domes. Most of the buildings are branches of the country's major banks or hotels. A central promenade features a pool and several statues and is the city's 'living room'. This is a great place to see Porto's many festivities and other celebrations.

☺ City Hall

Praça do General Humberto Delgado

Porto, 4049-001

PORTO TRAVEL GUIDE

Tel: +351 222 097 135

The City Hall overlooks the Avenue dos Aliados. From this palatial granite and marble building inspired by the municipal architecture of France and Flanders (also envisioned by Alvaro Siza Vieira) emerges a 70m high tower which is popular for the privileged view it offers from its top. From the top of the tower you can see the top of the hills of Vila Nova de Gaia on the other side of the Douro River. The City Hall holds guided tours every first and second Sundays of the month, from 10 to 11.30am.

In front of the building is a statue of Almeida Garret, a renowned Portuguese writer, and further down is Liberty Square (Praça da Liberdade), where a statue of King Pedro IV on a horse is located.

🌍 Clérigos Tower

Rua de S. Filipe de Nery

Porto, 4050-546

Tel: +351 222 001 729

If you walk southwest from Avenida dos Aliados (avenue) through Rua dos Clérigos (street) and into Rua Senhor Filipe de Nery (street) you will find this baroque work envisioned by the Italian architect Nicolau Nasoni in the 18th century. It was the tallest tower in Portugal in 1763 when it was first completed (the holder of this title currently is Lisbon's Vasco da Gama Tower).

The Clérigos Tower is one of the emblematic landmarks of Porto, and the panoramic view over the city and the Douro River from its top is a big attraction for travelers who are fond of photography or who simply enjoy a good view. The steep flight of 240 steps is worth the effort for the final viewpoint 76m above the ground.

Back on the ground, next to the Tower are found the Cordoaria Gardens and the city's former prison, a Pombaline and Neoclassical building where today is located the Portuguese Center for Photography Museum.

🌐 Portuguese Center for Photography

Former Porto's Prison and Court of Appeal Building

Campo dos Mártires da Pátria

Porto, 4050-368

Tel: +351 220 046 300

http://www.cpf.pt/

If you climbed up to the top of the Clérigos Tower, you will see the former Prison and Court of Appeal Building of Porto, and you will be easily able to reach it when you return to earth. After you return from you climb up the 240 steps of Clérigos Tower, you simply walk a few meters southwest.

The Portuguese Center of Photography was created in 1997 by the Portuguese Ministry of Culture and is currently managed by the General Archives office. It is a service of historic importance and it promotes Porto's photographic heritage.

The programming at the Center consists of temporary exhibitions and a permanent display of rare photographic cameras. The CPF owns a collection of Frederick William

Flower's work. He was a Scotsman who spent a large part of his life in Porto in the eighteen hundreds and whose photos (many of them taken in Porto of the city) are Portugal's oldest.

The Portuguese Center of Photography houses a specialized library, which offers services of consultation and reproduction, a shop and a free guided tour service to both the exhibitions and the building itself; however, you must book in advance.

Budget Tips

🌐 Accommodation

Oporto Invictus Hostel

Rua das Oliveiras 73

Porto, 4050-449

Tel: +351 222 024 371

http://www.oportoinvictushostel.com/

Porto is known for its affordable hostels and Oporto Invictus is a great one. Prices are €15 per bed per night.

The hostel has private bathroom, games room, television room, free internet access and wi-fi, secure lockers, 24h hot showers, fully equipped kitchen, lounge room and a bar. Towel rentals are €1.

Aliados Hotel

Rua de Elísio de Melo 27

Porto, 4000-196

Tel: +351 222 004 853

http://hotelaliados.com/

Right in the heart of the city center and housed in a historic building providing panoramic views over the city and especially Avenida dos Aliados, the three-star Aliados Hotel is decorated in pleasant colors. Rooms are equipped with hair-dryer, air-conditioning, direct-line phone, automatic wake-up call, satellite television with 30 channels and Wi-Fi. Some of the hotel's facilities include parking, room service and facilities for meetings and events. Accommodation costs range from €45 to €95 per room with breakfast included.

BessaHotel

Rua Dr Marques de Carvalho 111

Porto, 4100-325

Tel: +351 226 050 000

http://bessahotel.com/

This four-star hotel surrounded by several highlights of

the city such as the Serralves Museum, Casa da Musica, City Park, Foz do Douro and others, was beautifully designed and decorated. It is perfect for a business stay or a romantic holiday with your partner. The BessaHotel rooms include a safety deposit box, air-conditioning, hairdryer, desk, bathroom with bathtub, satellite and pay flat-screen TV, mini-bar and telephone. The prices for a double standard room for two adults range from €48 to €57 room only, or €62 to €75 with breakfast included (per night). Other facilities at the hotel to make your stay enjoyable include the fitness center, parking and facilities for meetings and events.

🌐 Restaurants, Cafés & Bars

A Marina

Cais da Ribeira 29

Porto, 4050-510

Tel: +351 222 000 302

http://restauranteamarina.com/

One of the oldest restaurants in the city (since 1939) and located in the Ribeira World Heritage area of Porto, A Marina has been passing down the secrets of traditional Portuguese cuisine for four generations and providing the best hospitality to its customers.

To start choose from the variety of appetizers, costing from .40 cents to €7.50, such as bread, cheese, prosciutto, corn bread, tapas and seafood. The main courses are traditional Portuguese as well as Porto cuisine such as codfish, steak, veal, octopus, shellfish, pork, trout, etc. Main courses dishes cost between €8 and €14.50 except for the €30 dish 'Fish Parrilhada' which serves two. A Marina also owns a cellar with the best national wines.

Onda Tropical Burguer

Cristal Park Mall

Rua de D. Manuel II 81 Store 12-13

Porto, 4050-345

Tel: +351 226 092 115

http://tropicalburguer.com/

For fans of fast food who are not ready to try traditional

Portuguese food, Onda Tropical Burguer is a good compromise. Choose from typical burgers, pizzas, calzones and hot dogs, or try lasagna, pasta salad, or try some of the traditional Porto dishes, such as the trademark Francezinha burger with egg or the Brazilian Picanha steak. For dessert there's cake slices and ice cream, or choose from the crepes and waffles. Dishes are prepared with a tropical touch and the average price is €10.

Porto Beer

Avenida da Boavista 1245

Porto, 4100-130

Tel: +351 226 086 793

http://hotelportopalacio.com/restaurante-cervejaria-portobeer.html

Belonging to the five-star Porto Palácio Congress Hotel & Spa, this glamorous restaurant charges surprisingly low prices, with the average cost being about €14 for a main dish and the intimate atmosphere of its interior is delightful.

Decorated in delicate white, black and gold, it's the perfect place for either a lounge lunch in the outdoors or a romantic dinner on the first floor. The menu includes fresh salads, light and vegetarian food, traditional food and their variants to white meats and vegetarian. There are also ice creams and cocktails and many other delightful options which match perfectly the environment inside the Porto Beer.

Cufra Grill

Via do Castelo do Queijo 395 Store R21

Porto, 4100-429

Tel: +351 229 387 884

http://www.cufragrill.com/

Cufra Grill is located between the Foz beaches and the City Park and its transparent building allows the customers to appreciate both the delicious food as well as the view of the seashores of Foz do Douro.

Offering traditional food, the Cufra Grill's menu features seafood dishes such as Portuguese Bulhão Pato Clams, Stuffed Crab and Seafood Rice. Also available are fish dishes like Salmon, Hake, Octopus and Sea Bass as well as meat dishes including Ribs, Chops, Veal, Pork and

Porto's traditional Rojões. The cheaper dishes are around €12 and the most expensive mians are about €26.

🌐 Shopping

Don't forget to buy some regional handcrafted items as a souvenir from Porto to add a memory of Portugal to your home. Here are some good places to find them.

O Galo

Rua de Mouzinho da Silveira 68

Porto, 4050-416

Tel: +351 223 325 294

http://galeriaartesanatogalo.pai.pt/

From traditional rugs, to handcrafts of cork and wood, blankets, decorative ceramic items and woven, O Galo has it all when it comes to traditional handicraft and souvenirs. Selling regional items not only from Porto, but from all over the country, it might even make you want to come back and visit other parts of Portugal.

O Arco da Ribeira

Cais da Ribeira 18

Porto, 4050-509

Tel: +351 222 083 917

A visitor who likes dessert wine would not want to leave Porto without a bottle or two of Port in their luggage. If that's you, take a peek at the wide range of Ports at the Arco da Ribeira, a shop located at the heart of the wharf, which also sells chocolates, 100% handmade tapestry from Viana do Castelo (a seaside city, to the north of

Porto), gourmet products and the opportunity to taste

Port, Berry Liqueur and Nespresso coffee in small

chocolate cups. The store also offers a tasting room and

bike rental services.

A Vida Portuguesa

Rua Galeria de Paris 20

Porto, 4050-162

Tel: +351 222 022 105

With a beautiful staircase, entering the store is a pleasant

experience in itself. A bright range of souvenirs is

displayed on its shelves and tables, from bottles to

scarves, handcrafts to soaps. Most of them wrapped in

retro packages which give the shop an atmosphere from

the 19th century. The space was originally a textiles shop.

While searching for the perfect souvenir, you can also glance through the windows and enjoy a beautiful view of Clérigos Tower which is just around the corner.

Know Before You Go

🌍 Entry Requirements

By virtue of the Schengen agreement, travellers from other countries in the European Union do not need a visa when visiting Portugal. Travellers from the UK, Bulgaria, Croatia, Cyprus, Romania and Ireland are also exempted from needing a visa and visitors from Australia, Canada and the USA, do not require a visa, provided that their stay does not exceed 90 days. Travellers requiring a Schengen visa will be able to enter Portugal with it multiple times within a 6 month period, if their stay does not exceed 90 days. They may need to prove that they have sufficient funds available to cover the duration of their stay in Portugal. For a stay exceeding 90 days, non-EU visitors will need to apply for a temporary residence permit.

🌍 Health Insurance

Citizens of other EU countries as well as residents from Switzerland, Norway, Iceland and Liechtenstein and the UK are covered for health care in Portugal with the European Health Insurance Card (EHIC), which can be applied for free of charge. If you need a Schengen visa for your stay in Portugal, you will also be required to obtain proof of health insurance for the duration of your stay (that offers at least €37,500 coverage), as part of their visa application. Visitors from Canada or the USA should check whether their regular health insurance covers travel and arrange for extended health insurance if required.

🌏 Travelling with Pets

When travelling with pets from another country in the European Union, certain requirements have to be met. The animal will need to be microchipped and up to date on their rabies shots. Additionally you should have applied for a EU pet passport from your country of origin. If you are planning to visit Portugal from outside the European Union, a health certificate in English or Portuguese needs to be submitted by a certified vet. For the non-commercial transport of animals to Portugal from non-European Union countries, the relevant authority at the Portuguese point of entry needs to be informed in writing at least 48 hours in advance of the arrival of the animal.

🌏 Airports

Apart from the airports in Lisbon, Faro and Oporto, Portugal's busiest routes are to the islands of the Azores and the Canaries. **Lisbon Portela Airport** (LIS) is the busiest international airport in Portugal and connects travellers with its capital,

Lisbon. **Francisco de Sá Carneiro Airport** (OPO) near Oporto is Portugal's second busiest airport. It is a focus city for EasyJet and Ryanair. **Faro Airport** (FAO) is particularly busy during the summer months, when it provides access to the Algarve region. **Madeira Airport** (FNC), with its notoriously short runway, was once considered one of the most dangerous airports. Located in Santa Cruz near Funchal, it provides access to the island of Madeira from destinations in France, Germany, Finland, the Netherlands and the UK. Another important airport in the Azores is **Horta International Airport** (HOR), which provides a vital link to the archipelago's outlying islands, such as Flores and Corvo. **Santa Maria Airport** (SMA) on the island of Santa Maria in the Azores once served as an important hub for the facilitation of trans-Atlantic connections, particularly in the post-World War Two era. Although it has in recent years slipped into a more regional role, it still has amenities suitable for transatlantic aircraft.

🌎 Airlines

TAP Portugal is the flag-carrying airline of Portugal. Founded in 1946, it flies travellers to 88 different destinations in 38 countries including Amsterdam, Barcelona, Madrid, Berlin, Frankfurt, Munich, Oslo, Marrakech, Miami, Luanda, Maputo, Moscow, Casablanca, Panama and Rio de Janeiro. SATA Air

Açores is a small airline based in the Azores, which operates scheduled flights as a carrier of passengers, cargo and mail. In the late 1990s, it acquired OceanAir and renamed it SATA International. Sata provides scheduled flights connecting Ponta Delgada to Lisbon, Madeira Island and Porto and also operates trans-Atlantic routes to Faro and Toronto. Portugalia began operations as a regional airline in the 1980s, flying domestic routes within Portugal as well as to Italy, France, Spain, Germany and Morocco. It was acquired by TAP Portugal in 2006.

Lisbon Portela Airport serves as a hub for Portugalia and TAP Portugal, as well as White Airlines, which operates mainly chartered flights on behalf of Portuguese tour operators. It is also a focus city for EasyJet and Ryanair. SATA Air Açores and SATA International are based at João Paulo II Airport in the Azores.

🌐 Currency

The currency of Portugal is the Euro. It is issued in notes in denominations of €500, €200, €100, €50, €20, €10 and €5. Coins are issued in denominations of €2, €1, 50c, 20c, 10c, 5c, 2c and 1c.

🌐 Banking & ATMs

Using ATMs in Portugal to withdraw money is simple if your ATM card is compatible with the MasterCard/Cirrus or Visa/Plus networks. Portuguese ATM machines are also known as Multibanco and will be identified with the logo, MB. There is a good distribution of machines available throughout Portugal. In general ATMs will give you the most beneficial rate of exchange, although some bank groups may levy an additional fee on international transactions. European ATMs are configured for 4-digit PIN numbers.

🌐 Credit Cards

Visa and MasterCard are widely accepted in many Portuguese businesses. Some businesses also accept American Express and will indicate this by displaying its logo. Other credit cards valid in Portugal include Diners Club, Maestro, Europay and JCB. Credit cards issued in Europe are smart cards that that are fitted with a microchip and require a PIN for each transaction. If you still have an older magnetic strip card, you may find that some facilities are not configured to process your transaction. Do remember to advise your bank or credit card company of your travel plans before leaving home.

🌎 Tourist Taxes

The city of Lisbon introduced a tourist tax in 2015 which will charge visitors €1 per night for the first 7 days of their stay in Lisbon. The tax does not apply to minor children. A review of this policy is due in 2019.

🌎 Reclaiming VAT

If you are not from the European Union, you can claim back VAT (Value Added Tax) paid on your purchases in Portugal. The VAT rate in Portugal is 23 percent and this can be claimed back on your purchases, if certain conditions are met. Only purchases of €60 and over qualify for a VAT refund. You will be asked for proof (usually in the form of a passport) that your normal residence is outside the European Union. Participating shops will clearly display that they offer a VAT-free service. A form needs to be filled in by the shop assistant. At customs of your last port within the European Union (which need not be the place where you bought the goods), you should submit this form. The goods and sales invoice will be inspected before the form is stamped and approved.

🌐 Tipping Policy

A service fee is usually included in restaurant bills in Portugal, but it is accepted to leave an additional 5-10 percent gratuity. It is also customary to tip taxi drivers 5 to 10 percent of the fee.

🌐 Mobile Phones

Most EU countries, including Portugal uses the GSM mobile service. This means that most UK phones and some US and Canadian phones and mobile devices will work in Portugal. However, phones using the CDMA network will not be compatible. While you could check with your service provider about coverage before you leave, using your own service in roaming mode will involve additional costs. The alternative is to purchase a Portuguese SIM card to use during your stay in Portugal. Portugal has three mobile networks. They are MEO (formerly known as TMN), Vodafone and NOS (formerly known as Optimus). MEO is the largest service provider that offers the best coverage and SIM cards are available from €2.50. Data only rates begin at €10 for 10GB, valid for 3 days. Vodafone has a vendor at Porto airport and you can get a data only SIM card for €2.50 or voice and data. The data rate begins at €1.99 for 100 Mb. Bear in mind that for the data only package there are two different rates, a 7 day rate and a 30 day rate, which cannot be interchanged. NOS is the smallest of the Portuguese networks. They offer a SIM card for €2.50, with various top-up packages ranging from €1.99 for 30 MB that expires within 24 hours to €7.99 for 1 GB that is valid for one month.

🌐 Dialling Code

The international dialling code for Portugal is +351.

🌐 Emergency Numbers

Police: 112

Medical Emergencies: 112

Fire Rescue: 112

Forest Fires: 117

24 Hour Health line for emergencies: 808 242 424

Sea Rescue: 214 401 919

Maritime Police: 210 911 100

MasterCard: 800 811 272

Visa: 800 811 107

🌐 Public Holidays

1 January: New Year's Day

March/April: Good Friday

25 April: Freedom Day

1 May: Worker's Day

10 June: Portugal Day

15 August: Feast of the Assumption

8 December: Immaculate Conception

25 December: Christmas Day

🌐 Time Zone

In the winter season from the end of October to the end of March, Portugal's official time is the same as Greenwich Mean Time/Coordinated Universal Time (GMT/UTC); Eastern Standard Time (North America) -4; Pacific Standard Time (North America) -7.

🌐 Daylight Savings Time

Clocks are set forward one hour on the last Sunday of March and set back one hour on the last Sunday of October for Daylight Savings Time.

🌐 School Holidays

The academic year in Portugal begins in mid September and ends in mid June, but there may be different schedules for private and international schools. The summer holiday is from mid June to mid September, although the exact times may vary according to region. There are short breaks between Christmas and New Year and also during Easter and for the Carnival season in February or March.

🌐 Trading Hours

Most shops in Portugal trade from 9am to 7pm on weekdays and until 1pm on Saturdays, but at some shopping centers, trading hours may be extended to midnight. Shops may also stay open on Saturday afternoons and even Sundays during the Christmas season. Certain shops close for lunch between 1 and 3pm. Banks are open from 8.30am to 3pm on weekdays and the post office is open from 9am to 6pm, Monday to Friday, with extended weekend hours available in at some branches, for example at the airport. Pharmacies trade from 9am to 7pm, but details about the nearest all night pharmacy will usually also be signposted.

🌎 Driving Laws

The Portuguese drive on the right hand side of the road. A driver's licence from any of the European Union member countries is valid in Portugal. If visiting from a non-EU country, you will need to obtain an International Driving Permit to be able to drive in Portugal. The minimum driving age in Portugal is 18. The speed limit in Portugal is 120km per hour for freeways, 90km per hour for rural roads and 50km per hour in urban areas. The alcohol limit in Portugal is below 0.5 g/l. Toll roads in Portugal can be paid at dispensing booths or alternately, you could obtain a permanent or temporary electronic device that will be identified as a toll pass. This can be paid via credit card or ATM. Children under the age of 12 are not allowed to ride in the front seat. It is also illegal to drive with head phones or when using a mobile phone. Make sure that the vehicle you are using is up to date on road tax, fully covered by third party insurance and carries standard emergency gear such as warning triangles and a reflective safety vest. If older than four years, the car needs to have a valid IPO (Inspecção Periódica Obrigatória) as proof of roadworthiness.

🌏 Drinking Laws

In Portugal, the legal purchase age is 16 for beer and wine and 18 for spirits. The sale of alcohol in bars and restaurants is forbidden after midnight and public drinking after 2am.

🌏 Smoking Laws

In 2008, smoking was banned in all public places in Portugal, including work spaces, public transport, schools, libraries, museums, indoor car parks, indoor sports facilities, bars, cafes and discos. Restaurants with a floor space exceeding 100 sq. m. can allocate an enclosed area of not more than 30 percent with adequate ventilation as a smoker's area. The minimum age for smoking is 18. Persons who violate anti-smoking laws can be liable for a fine of between €50 and €750.

🌏 Electricity

Electricity: 230 volts

Frequency: 50 Hz

Portuguese electricity sockets are compatible with the Type C Euro adaptor and Type F plugs, which features two round pins or prongs. If travelling from the USA, you will need a power converter or transformer to convert the voltage from 230 to 110, to avoid damage to your appliances. The latest models of many laptops, camcorders, mobile phones and digital cameras are dual-voltage with a built in converter.

🌍 Tourist Information (TI)

There are several tourist information outlets in Lisbon, the capital. The Lisbon Welcome Center is at 15 Rua do Arsenal, but there is also a tourist information outlet at Lisbon Portela Airport and Palacio Foz, in Praca dos Restauradores. The Cascais tourist information office is at Rua Visconde da Luz and there is also a tourist information outlet at Avenue Miguel Bombarda in Sintra. The Porto Convention Bureau at Ponte Luís I promotes tourism in Porto.

🌍 Food & Drink

Fish and seafood are important ingredients of Portuguese cuisine. One of the most popular dishes is bacalhau or salted cod, which can be found in a huge selection of regional varieties. Sardines - grilled or fried, is another national favorite and makes common street food in Lisbon, particularly in June when the Santa Antonio festival takes place. The traditional Portuguese soup is Caldo Verde, with a base of onion and potato and another signature dish is feijoada, a rich and meaty bean stew. Chouriço is a Portuguese pork sausage similar to the Spanish chorizo and it has a kosher counterpart in alheira de mirandela. Originally devised by Iberian Jews to fool the Inquisitors, the sausage may include veal, rabbit, chicken and duck.

Try Caldeirada de Enguias or eel stew from Aveiro or the seafood stew cataplana from the Algarve. In Porto, try the francesinha, a sandwich stuffed with ham, sausage and steak, smothered in cheese and then served with a signature tomato based sauce. The island of Madeira has plenty to offer, gastronomically speaking, ranging from meaty Espetada to Bolo de Mel or honey cake. The Azores boasts a selection of dairy products, including the well-known Queijo da Ilha which originates from the island, São Jorge. Here, too, seafood is popular, particularly octopus, mackerel and lamprey. Enjoy home-grown pineapples and the one-pot speciality cozida on São Miguel, while a slow-cooked Alcatra pot-roast may tantalize your taste buds on Terçeira. Azorean sweets include Massa Sovada or Portuguese sweet bread, and Malasadas.

Port wine, also known as Vinho de Porto, is a sweet, fortified wine made of red grapes grown exclusively in the Douro Valley of northern Portugal. It is traditionally enjoyed after dinner and served with cheese. Madeira is famous for wines such as Bual, Sercial, Malmsey and Verdelho. You should also try Poncho, a drink made from sugarcane rum, lemon juice and honey or ginja, a local liqueur distilled from cherries. Nikita, a blend of pineapple and vanilla can be enjoyed with or without alcohol. Try the distinctive wines from Såo Miguel and Pico in the Azores.

🌎 Websites

https://www.visitportugal.com/en

http://portugal.com/

http://wikitravel.org/en/Portugal

http://www.insideportugaltravel.com/

http://www.portugal-live.com/

http://www.portugal-live.net/

http://www.travel-in-portugal.com/

Printed in Great Britain
by Amazon